Real People

Ellen Ochoa

By Pamela Walker

Children's Press
A Division of Scholastic Inc.
New York / Toronto / London / Auckland / Sydney
Mexico City / New Delhi / Hong Kong
Danbury, Connecticut

Photo Credits: Cover and all photos courtesy of Johnson Space Center, NASA
Contributing Editor: Jennifer Silate
Book Design: Victoria Johnson

Library of Congress Cataloging-in-Publication Data

Walker, Pamela, 1958-
 Ellen Ochoa / by Pamela Walker.
    p. cm. -- (Real people)
   Includes bibliographical references.
   ISBN 0-516-23433-1 (lib. bdg.) -- ISBN 0-516-23587-7 (pbk.)
   1. Ochoa, Ellen -- Juvenile literature. 2. Women astronauts--United States--
Biography--Juvenile literature. 3. Hispanic Americans in the professions--Juvenile literature. 4. Hispanic
American women--Biography--Juvenile literature. [1. Ochoa, Ellen. 2. Astronauts. 3. Hispanic
Americans--Biography. 4. Women--Biography.] I. Title.

TL789.85.025 W35 2001
629.45'0092--dc21

                                                                            2001017267

Contents

ROMINGER HUSBAND
PAYETTE   TOKAPEB
JERNIGAN OCHOA BARRY

5

Ellen had to **train** to be an astronaut.

FULL FUSELAGE TRAINER

7

Ellen had to learn how to use many **machines**.

She worked hard, but she had fun.

11

Ellen was part of a team with other astronauts.

13

When Ellen finished her training, she went into **space**.

14

15

In space, Ellen did many important jobs.

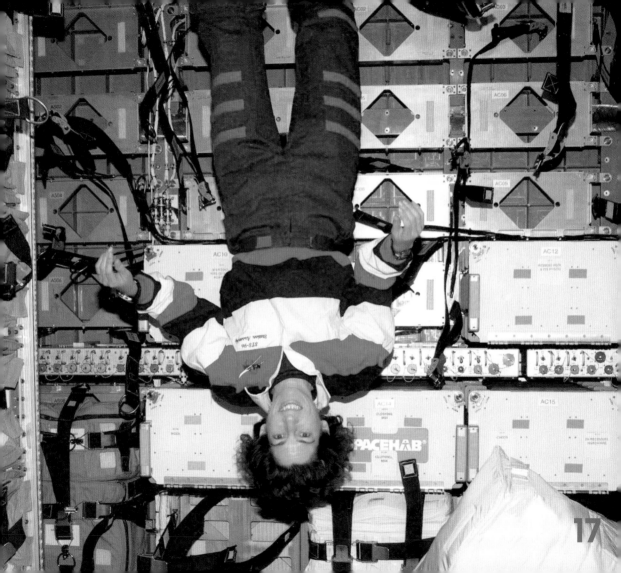

17

Ellen has been in space three times!

Ellen talks to people about being an astronaut.

She tells them to work hard.

If they do, they could be astronauts, too.

21

New Words

astronaut (**as**-truh-naht) a person who travels into space

machines (muh-**sheenz**) devices that work

space (**spays**) the area between planets and stars

train (**trayn**) to learn through practice

To Find Out More

Books
Ellen Ochoa: The First Hispanic Woman Astronaut
by Maritza Romero
The Rosen Publishing Group

Astronauts Today
by Rosanna Hansen
Random House

Web Sites
Women of Space
http://www.friends-partners.org/~mwade/articles/womspace.htm
Learn more about other famous women who have traveled into
space at this Web site.

Famous Hispanics: Ellen Ochoa
http://coloquio.com/famosos/ellenoch.html
This Web site includes a brief biography of Ellen Ochoa,
NASA's first Hispanic woman astronaut.

Index

About the Author
Pamela Walker was born in Kentucky. When she grew up, she moved to New York and became a writer.

Reading Consultants
Kris Flynn, Coordinator, Small School District Literacy, The San Diego County Office of Education

Shelly Forys, Certified Reading Recovery Specialist, W.J. Zahnow Elementary School, Waterloo, IL

Sue McAdams, Former President of the North Texas Reading Council of the IRA, and Early Literacy Consultant, Dallas, TX